Make A Will, Do It Right!

Or The One You Don't Like Will End Up With All Your Stuff!

Vernita C. Williams, Esq.
Miami Probate & Estate Planning Lawyer

Jacobs & Whitehall
73-03 Bell Blvd, #10
Oakland Gardens, NY 11364
www.jacobsandwhitehall.com

Ordering Information:

Quantity sales. Special discounts are available on quantity purchases by corporations, associations, and others. For details, contact the publisher at the address above.

Orders by U.S. trade bookstores and wholesalers. Please contact Jacobs & Whitehall: Tel: (888) 570-7338 or visit www.jacobsandwhitehall.com.

Printed in the United States of America.

Published in 2020

Book Cover Design
Chelae Cummings of The BluPen, LLC
www.theblupen.com

ISBN: 978-1-946481-53-5

DEDICATIONS

This book is dedicated to my mother, Juanita D. Scott, my glimpse of God's unconditional love.

****

In loving memory of my father, Claude J. Williams, who loved me until I became his daughter, again.

****

To Brigette, my cousin who is my little sister and my big sister too. (It depends upon what we are talking about!) To Nia Pie too, my little cousin who has taught me so much from the day she was born.

****

To Jesse, my husband, the gospel preacher. Though my estate planning seminars have little to do with preaching, you have attended more estate planning seminars than anyone else and championed this cause by the recording, editing and internet posting of my estate planning videos, and other material, in support of my life's work. Thank you Jesse. What a difference you've made in my life!

****

ACKNOWLEDGEMENTS

I have had the pleasure of working as an attorney in South Florida for at least two decades. Each case was unique and with each case came the opportunity to see the law through the eyes of the people I have served. I have learned, not just how the law plays itself out in the courtroom, but how it affects the individual. Most importantly, I have come to know what is important to the people I have served in ways that I never knew, until after I spent time with them in the trenches, in the legal battle, fighting for them. As I reflect upon my years of service, I am grateful:

- To my Pastor, Bishop Victor T. Curry, and my home church, Miami, Florida's New Birth Baptist Cathedral of Faith International, for hosting one of my first community estate planning seminars and being a tremendous source of encouragement
- To all the South Florida churches and groups that hosted my estate planning seminars

- To every client who presented a new fact pattern that caused me to dig deeper, research longer, become more resilient or in some way carve a unique pathway to victory
- To my law office staff for their tireless assistance in serving my clients and providing community seminars
- To the many friends and supporters who helped in countless ways, giving suggestions, feedback, ideas, and sometimes just a listening ear; and especially to Francina Bolden, Karen Marshall, Abdul El Amin, Ann Lowry, Pamela Shuler and my Stewardship Ministry co-laborers Wayne Dean, Patrecia Ricketts, Theresa Rolle, Tommye L. Bell, Brenda Jackson and Tara Davis. You all are priceless!
- To my editor, E. Claudette Freeman, thank you for your editorial help and especially for keeping me from being "too academic." You are brilliant!
- To the Probate Judges of the 11th Judicial Circuit in and for Miami Dade County, Florida for the contributions you have made to my professional development and to the stories in this book. A special thanks to Judge Maria Korvick, Judge Yvonne Colodny, Judge Celeste H.

Muir, Judge Rosa C. Figarola, Judge Jorge E. Cueto, Judge Mindy S. Glazer, Judge Arthur L. Rothenberg, Judge Bernard Shapiro, Judge Gerald Bagley, Judge Michael Genden, Judge Norman S. Gerstein, Judge Lawrence A. Schwartz and Judge Gerald Hubbart. Your rulings have given true meaning to the law and how it applies to each fact pattern. I have many endearing stories of what I learned and experienced practicing before you. Each of you have added value to my life and I am eternally grateful.

DISCLAIMER

This publication is intended to be used for educational purposes only. No legal advice is being given, and no attorney-client relationship is created by reading this material. The author assumes no liability for any errors or omissions or for how this book or its contents are used or interpreted or for any consequences resulting directly or indirectly from the use of this book. For legal or any other advice, please consult an experienced attorney or the appropriate expert who is aware of the specific facts of your case and is knowledgeable of the law in your jurisdiction.

Vernita C. Williams, Esq., PA
6625 Miami Lakes Drive, 3rd Floor
Miami, FL 33014
www.attorneyvernitawilliams.com
www.vcwlaw.com
786-831-9483

TABLE OF CONTENTS

INTRODUCTION

You accepted your stepchildren and raised them as your own. You gave them the same love and care you gave your biological children. But your untimely death left your marital home to your husband. Well, that seems fine. Right? Well, here is where the dead may want to rise! Your husband gave your property to his children who are your stepchildren. Had you known he would do such a thing, excluding your children, you never would have placed your husband on the deed to your property! Now your biological children are in court, hopelessly scrambling and scratching, trying to find a legal basis to somehow inherit your property. Can you imagine that?

Or ponder this. You are deathly ill and the people you least want to see are coming to your bedside, guessing about your ailment and how much longer you have. You are too sick to do anything about this and you wonder why those who know better don't ban the curiosity seekers from putting in these mocking appearances!

What about this frequent occurrence? You wrote a Will, but the court threw it out! You did not execute it according to state laws. How could you? You didn't even know anything about state laws concerning Wills. Or, you didn't write a Will and now it is chaos because your unknown children, (the ones you never told your known children about), have surfaced to fight over your estate. Worst of all, your known children are now forced to share with your so-called illegitimate children because at least one of those children has a birth certificate with your name on it! Oh, can you image what the conversations at the next family reunion will be concerning that!

These things are unthinkable! You would never knowingly let these things happen! But they happen all the time. This is why you need to do a Last Will & Testament and other things to get your affairs in order. I admit. Writing a Will is not the most fun thing to think about or do. Besides, you have been too busy trying to live to think about dying. And as far as you can see, death is something that has been happening to other people, right? Since nobody is bothering you about this now, you keep planning to get around to it someday.

You are not alone. Statistics show that as many as 75% of Americans do not have a Will or any kind of estate plan. Even world renown Queen of Soul, Aretha Franklin, died intestate, as reported by CNN's Faith Karimi, in the August 2018 article on the network's website, "Aretha Franklin Had No Will Or Trust At The Time Of Death." Aretha had four sons and you would think that the estate distribution strategy should be a simple division of everything between them. But estates, especially large ones, are seldom so simply settled. Although Danielle and Andy Mayoras, Personal Finance Contributors to Forbes Magazine online, noted that the family was pulling together to protect her legacy, they have a hard fight ahead. The Mayoras' August 2018 article indicated that after everybody who conjures up a reason Aretha should give them money comes forth, her estimated $80,000,000 estate may provide plenty of fodder for lawsuits and IRS battles for years to come.

News Flash! News Flash! Aretha died in August 2018 and was thought to not have a Last Will & Testament. But apparently things have changed! A June 2019 article, "Tension Developing in Aretha Franklin Will Dispute," published by the Associated Press is a sneak preview of things to come. The developments suggest that a 2014 handwritten Will found under cushions in Aretha's Detroit home named her youngest son, Kecalf Franklin, as the personal representative and not her niece who has been appointed. Some say Kecalf is not qualified. Nevertheless, Kecalf is demanding his appointment as personal representative, stating that the handwritten Will names him, and that the niece has not given him full disclosure of the value of his mother's assets. Although several news sources report that the Queen of Soul wrote several handwritten versions of a

Will, so far none of the Wills have been authenticated and accepted by the court. Well, the circus has begun! Only God knows how this will end!

Aretha is not the only one with a tumultuous estate. Surprisingly, pop icon Prince didn't have a Will, a fact that has created much turmoil. You would think that he would have had this vital estate document considering he was known to file a lawsuit at the drop of a hat. The Hollywood Reporter once said of Prince in the April 2016 article, "Prince's Legal Legacy: Contract Fights, Copyright Battles and Changing His Name," that the artist's legal skirmishes are nearly as legendary as the music. That same report noted that while Prince was quite diligent when it came to his music business, the same may not have been so true when it came to his personal life. When he died, survived by no wife and no children, people came from everywhere to stake their claim. Prince's posthumous suitors who bid to be named "heir" included everything from an alleged secret wife to a prison inmate who claimed to be his love child. After his death, People Magazine reporters Jeff Nelson and Jordan Runtagh compiled what could easily be titled

WHO WANTS PRINCE'S MONEY. That list included alleged family members, as well as businesses and individuals claiming to be owed money.

At least 29 cases of people claiming to be an heir have been dismissed by the court, according to a July 2016 Business Insider article, leaving one whole sister and five half siblings who are likely to be declared actual heirs. This won't happen overnight since some of the folk who were denied "heirship" have filed an appeal to have their denials reviewed and reversed. This makes for a long road ahead for Prince's family.

Not all celebrities made the mistake of not executing a Last Will and Testament. The King of Pop, Michael Jackson, had a Will but his family thought he didn't. They prematurely filed court documents that they later withdrew when Michael's Will was discovered. It turned out that Michael gave everything to his mother and three children, leaving his tyrannical father, Joe Jackson, to manage a plain old ordinary life with far less financial support than he thought he deserved. Kamika Dunlap's November 2009 article on Findlaw.com, "The

Michael Jackson Will: Father Gets No Inheritance" explains the elder Mr. Jackson had no room to contest the Will since he was not an heir.

Sadly, and although Michael had a Will, his estate has been plagued by tax court issues since 2013. Michael's administrators argued that his estate was bankrupt at the time of his death and only worth about $2000. But the Tax Court thought differently, based on Billboard magazine, saying that Michael's likeness, posthumous earnings and massive influence warranted an estate value assessment of more than $400,000,000 with hefty associated taxes. Eriq Gardner's 2016 article in the magazine detailed a variety of taxing financial possibilities. Not only that, a considerable number of lawsuits involving Michael's estate have been filed. Some lawsuits stem from accusations that music released posthumously was produced with voices other than Michael's. Other lawsuits, against people using Michael's image without permission, have been filed by the estate. Although the King of Pop is gone, his estate is yet alive, unsettled, still making money and engaging in lawsuits.

The Godfather of Soul, James Brown, also had a Will. Strangely, his Will dictated that his estate be run by a committee of three estate representatives who would manage estate matters by majority vote. Byte of Prevention Blogger Jay Reeves wrote in his March 2015 article, "Nobody Feels Good About James Brown's Estate," that the committee disintegrated in short order as members left amidst accusations of misappropriation of estate funds. Some say Brown's estate was worth less than $5,000,000 while others say, based upon earnings from continued use of his image and music, his estate is worth as much as $100,000,000. New York Times Reporter Steve Knopper's February 2018 investigative work, "Why Is James Brown's Estate Still Unsettled? Ask the Lawyers," notes a lot of the discord may be related to legal wrangling. Since Brown's death in 2006, not a dime of his estate has been distributed as scholarships to underprivileged children according to his wishes. His estate has been held up by at least a dozen related lawsuits.

One lawsuit was filed by his wife, Tommie Rae Hynie who, although she allegedly and knowingly signed a prenuptial agreement agreeing she wouldn't get anything, still filed a lawsuit to stake her claim to the estate. Some of James Brown's children fought her, saying that she could not have been married to their father because when they married, she was still married to a man whom she married to help get his immigration papers. Well, a South Carolina court said that Hynie's marriage to the immigrant was invalid because the immigrant already had a wife in his native country! Writing for the New York Times in January 2015, Larry Rohter wonderfully recorded the details of two questionable marriages. Since Hynie's immigration marriage was no good, the court reasoned that she was available to marry when she wed James Brown. According to Rohter's "Judge Rules Tommie Rae Hynie Brown Was Married to James Brown," this meant she was a legitimate wife but one with a prenuptial agreement that said she gets nothing! Wonder how this will turn out? I guess the Godfather of Soul is turning in his grave!

Whether they did a Will or not, the Queen of Soul, Pop Icon Prince, the King of Pop and the Godfather of Soul will undoubtedly all have tax issues lurking around the corner. Their fame and posthumous earnings will inevitably create tax liabilities. They all may be posthumously singing the blues as it looks like their estates will not be settled anytime soon.

You may not be famous with a lot of people hanging on the coattail of your estate for money, but you still need to do an estate plan. If you are among those who would rather walk across hot coals barefoot than sit down with an attorney and write a Will, you may be creating plenty of problems for your loved ones when you die. You should care enough about your relatives to not leave your affairs in a sham, forcing them to deal with the agony of straightening a mess that could cost time in years of legal proceedings and cost plenty of money in legal fees.

Why Did I Write This Book?

As an estate planning attorney, I have seen it all. I have been through horrendous situations. I have received a call from a dying mother who urged me to make sure her no good son got nothing from her estate.

I have represented someone whose brother, while she mourned in front of their mother's open casket, physically attacked her. I have received a call from a hospital administrator asking me to advise her concerning who is entitled to visit a terminally ill patient in hospice after that administrator had an unruly son escorted from his dying mother's bedside by the police. When it comes to Last Wills and Estates, you name it, I've dealt with it. Much of the drama could have been avoided if people planned their estates and did so properly. But then again, some people are going to do drama whether you have a proper estate plan or not! Just don't let it be that the drama lives and grows because you failed to plan properly.

To circumvent problems, I want to help you figure out what you need to do and how you need to do it. You have a right to put the person you want in charge of your affairs and to transfer property to the person you want to have it. Not doing an estate plan or doing things incorrectly can create a lot of problems, confusion, heartache, needless expenses, and ultimately cause property to end up with someone you never would have given it to. Think about that. That person who you cannot stand, who you know has no integrity, and is more prone to criminal enterprise than a hard day's work can potentially end up with your home and everything in your estate because you did not take the time to execute paperwork that spells out your legacy. Are you getting a vivid picture of how important Wills and estate planning are?

How To Use This Book

The purpose of this book is to help you think about estate planning and what you fear may happen after you pass away. I want you to think about how to prevent your worst nightmares from becoming reality for loved ones. This book will help you understand key questions you should answer to define what you want to do.

When you consider your estate plan, you should plan in two specific areas: INCAPACITY PLANNING and ESTATE PLANNING. Incapacity planning spells out who will help you if you are alive but can't do things for yourself. Estate planning describes how your estate will be handled and who will get your assets if you have passed away. Incapacity Planning and Estate Planning are not just for rich people. Proper planning is for anyone who wants to have personal order in their lives, wants to alleviate confusion, wants to put the right people in charge of their estate and wants to give their assets to the people of their choosing.

The strategy that I give you in this book will guide you as you answer eight specific questions related to these two planning areas:

Area One: Incapacity Planning

- Decision 1: Do you need a living will?
- Decision 2: Do you need a medical power of attorney?
- Decision 3: Do you need a durable power of attorney?

Area Two: Estate Planning

- Decision 4: Do you need a last will and testament?
- Decision 5: Do you need a revocable trust?
- Decision 6: Do you need a joint tenancy deed?
- Decision 7: Do you need a Totten trust?

- Decision 8: Do you need life insurance?

When you answer these and related questions you will find in this book, you will have a comprehensive idea about what you need to put in place and what you need to discuss with your attorney. This book will help you consider some things that you have never thought about and help you develop a detailed and well thought out plan tailored to meet your specific needs.

How To Plan Your Estate

You should create your estate plan based on the decisions derived from the eight questions introduced. In the decision making process in which you will consult an estate planning attorney (and this may sound funny), you should act without any diplomacy whatsoever! Be very candid with your lawyer about the people in the family, the people you don't like, the people you don't want to get things and the people you do want to get things. Be honest about who you do not trust and let the attorney know the people you think are best suited for positions such as executor of your estate or trustee of a revocable trust. Your doctor cannot diagnose and prescribe the right treatment if you are not honest about what is going on with your body. Likewise, your lawyer cannot help you create the best plan if you are not completely honest about what is going on in your family. Be honest, even if the truth is embarrassing or does not place you or your family in a good light. Listen to the attorney's advice and make sure the attorney you use is experienced in estate planning and has a keen understanding of how the documents prepared will work in probate court.

Decision 1

Do You Need A Living Will?

He seemed awfully mean-spirited. What kind of husband was he? How could he do this? There he was, fighting his wife's parents for years. All they wanted was to give their daughter medical treatment and a chance to live. He, the husband, wanted to disconnect his wife's life support. Well, he eventually did just that! And when his wife died, he cremated her. The most her parents got from him was a fax - after the memorial was over - saying where their daughter's ashes were!

The Story Of Terri Schiavo

For many who followed this gripping story, it was confusing, disheartening and even infuriating. No matter how spectators felt, they heard questions that demanded answers. Would you want to be on life support? Would you want your family to do legal battle for a decade while you lay helpless, waiting for a court decision as to whether you should remain on life support? So important was this issue that even then Florida Governor Jeb Bush and then US President George W. Bush weighed in, bringing national attention to the case of Terri Schiavo, the woman at the center of this controversy.

According to "Facts, Lies and Videotapes: The Permanent Vegetative State and The Sad Case of Terri Schiavo," a Summer 2005 article in The Journal of Law, Medicine & Ethics, this 15-year saga started in February 1990 when then 26-year-old Terri Schiavo, compromised by diet related electrolyte imbalances, went into cardiac arrest and was resuscitated. The USA Today reported, in its February 2005 article, "Schiavo Case Highlights Eating Disorders," that one of Terri's doctors was blamed and sued for Terri's diet related electrolyte imbalance and ultimately paid two million dollars to settle the malpractice suit. Whatever the case, this medical calamity left Terri severely brain damaged. Although doctors said Terri Schiavo was in a persistent vegetative state with no hope for recovery, Terri's parents insisted that she could be rehabilitated, securing a variety of treatments for Terri which proved unsuccessful according to a November 2014 report titled "Schiavo Timeline, Part 1" published by the University of Miami Ethics Program.

Meanwhile according to Terri's Florida Supreme Court case file and the state guardianship case file, Terri's husband who was initially amicable with Terri's parents and in agreement with treatment attempts, begin to declare that Terri would never want to live in such a vegetative state and demanded that Terri receive no life support. He also demanded that she be allowed to move, without further delay, into her fate of inevitable death. Terri's husband ultimately prevailed. His victory was only after the circus drama of having a court order on at least two separate occasions to discontinue Terri's feeding tube only to have the feeding tube reinserted. One of those decisions was at the behest of the Florida Congress which worked through the weekend to achieve this end. A detailed description of all the phases of this 15-year old legal battle can be found in Wikipedia under "Terri Schiavo Case."

Why was Terri Schiavo's husband fighting so hard? Was it true that her husband had gotten her medical malpractice suit money, gotten a new woman with whom he had fathered a child and moved on with his life? Was the husband a monster? Or was he understandably tired of seeing his wife in such condition and having his life on hold? Why didn't he divorce Terri, give her incapacitated non-responsive being back to her parents and move on with his new woman? Was it because if he divorced her he could not, in clear conscious, justify keeping the malpractice suit money? Was the best financial option for the husband to remove life support so that he could be the surviving husband entitled to keep the lawsuit money? Was the quest to remove the feeding tube really about Terri Schiavo's wishes or was it about the husband's economic future?

Terri was 26 years old when she went into cardiac arrest. She had no living will, nor any other document that dealt with death and dying. Her husband, plagued by suspicions of greed and questionable motives, insisted that his young wife had told him she would never want to be on life support. Though few people believed a seemingly healthy young woman would have taken occasion to give her husband life support instructions, the husband litigated relentlessly, claiming to carry out a pledge to keep this "no life support" promise to his wife. Terri's husband insisted that her life ended on February 25, 1990, the day she went into cardiac arrest, rather than March 31, 2005, when she died 15 years later after her feeding tube was removed.

After Terri died, she was cremated. However, Terri's parents complained that the husband did not tell them the time or place Terri's ashes were to be buried although he was ordered by court to do so. A June 2005 Associated Press article captured it best, "Schiavo's Remains Buried Amid Acrimony: Acrimony Between Terri Schiavo's Parents and Husband Continues as Her Remains Buried in Florida." According to the article, Terri's parents were notified of the burial of her ashes by fax only after the memorial service had already taken place.

The vitriol between this husband and his wife's parents is captured on the wife's tombstone which has two different dates of death. The epitaph, easily construed as one sarcastic last dig at Terri's parents, reads:

SCHIAVO

THERESA MARIE

BELOVED WIFE

Born December 3, 1963

Departed This Earth

February 25, 1990

At Peace March 31, 2005

I Kept My Promise

Note that Terri died on March 31, 2005. Six days before her death, Attorney George Felos filed in the Supreme Court of the United States, "Respondent Michael Schiavo's Opposition To Application For Injunction," Case No. 04A-825, in which the husband made a final demand that Terri be allowed to die without the re-insertion of the feeding tube. He summarized what a fiasco the case had been, his assessment quite revealing! It was true. By the time Terri was buried, the Schiavo saga had lasted 15 years; involved 14 appeals and numerous motions, petitions and hearings in Florida courts; created five suits in federal district court; caused extensive political unconstitutional interventions through the Florida state legislature (led by Governor Jeb Bush and ultimately unsuccessful); sparked interventions through the U.S. Congress (led by President George W. Bush) and led to four denied appeals to the Supreme Court of the United States. After all that, I ask you: Was that any kind of way to live? Was it right for Terri? Terri's husband? Terri's parents? What could have made this process shorter? Surely they did not need 15 years to figure this out!

What You Should Know About Life Support

Most life support decisions are not as gut wrenching and do not last as long as the Terri Schiavo case. However, any of us could be faced with life support decisions, be they our own or involving a loved one. For this reason, it is best to think things through before a crisis.

Terri Schiavo's case was about whether she should be on life support. When the phrase life support is used, many people think of a breathing machine. However, Terri's life support was not about a breathing machine because she could breathe on her own. Terri could not eat on her own; so, she received food and water by a feeding tube. This is why it is important to understand that life support entails far more than whether you want to be on a breathing machine. Life support considerations also include whether you want cardiac resuscitation or CPR, whether you want a feeding tube to feed you artificially if you cannot eat on your own, whether you want blood transfusions, or if you want surgery or invasive diagnostic tests, dialysis, or antibiotics.

Crudely stated, Terri's family was faced with deciding whether they wanted to starve her to death by withholding food and water. After 15 years, Terri's husband won the legal battle to remove her feeding tube. On March 31, 2005 Terri died, dehydrated and starved.

What Is A Living Will & How Does It Relate To Life Support?

Remember that life support is the use of artificial and other measures to keep a person alive. These measures include mechanical respiration or a breathing machine, cardiac resuscitation, a feeding tube, blood or blood products, surgery or invasive diagnostic tests, kidney dialysis and antibiotics. The living will is a simple document that states whether you want to be on any of these life support measures if it is determined that you are not able to live without these artificial measures. The medical power of attorney is a document that names and gives authority to the person you would like to make medical decisions for you if you cannot. Sometimes, particularly in healthcare settings, the medical power of attorney and the living will are combined into a document called advanced directives. Whatever you do, be sure to tell your medical power of attorney your thoughts about whether you want to be on life support. This is extremely important as your medical power of attorney should not have to guess about what you want and should not have to bear the responsibility of making the decisions alone without your input.

Questions You Should Ponder Before Preparing A Living Will

There are seven questions you should think about and answer so that you can draft a living will that tells your loved ones exactly what you want and don't want.

All of these things should be specifically accepted or rejected when doing a living will.

1. Do you want mechanical respiration or a breathing machine? If you think a breathing machine for a short duration such as two to four weeks is appropriate, then say so. If you want a designated person to decide after a certain period you should say this as well.
2. Do you want cardiac resuscitation? This measure to start the heart beating again is called CPR. It is done when a person's heart stops beating. If you believe administering CPR once or twice in the same day is good, then state that. However, if you believe that you would prefer a do not resuscitate order if you are having multiple CPR sessions in a day, then state that. Use caution in making this decision. Most people are willing to be resuscitated once or twice in a day.
3. Do you want a feeding tube, or any other artificial or invasive measure used for nutrition and hydration? Even if you are brain dead you may be able to breathe on your own. If you are in a vegetative state because you are brain dead, but you can breathe on your own, do you want the withholding of food and

water so that you can experience death by starvation and dehydration?

4. Do you want blood or blood products if needed? This is often refused by certain religions such as Jehovah Witnesses.
5. Do you want any form of surgery or invasive diagnostic tests? Most people who have not had a long history of illness approve of surgery and diagnostic tests. However, some people, particularly those who have battled a debilitating disease for many years, are prepared to accept the consequences of no further surgery or diagnostic tests. Where are your thoughts in this regard?
6. Do you want kidney dialysis? Some people refuse kidney dialysis because they are in denial about their failed renal condition and the consequences of not doing dialysis. Others understand the need for dialysis but choose not to have it, not being able to embrace having a port placed in their body for dialysis and not wanting to accommodate the intrusions of the dialysis process which often requires two or three doctor visits per week.

7. Do you want antibiotics? While the average person would not refuse an antibiotic course of therapy, terminally ill people who have struggled for years may. Are you at a point where you are so tired of the struggle of your medical condition that you don't want any more antibiotic treatments if you get a viral or bacterial infection?

Decision 2

Do You Need A Medical Power Of Attorney?

When I became an attorney, I expected to deal with lofty things - things that were deep, noble and profound. I didn't expect to deal with unseemly behavior in hospitals and midnight phone calls from hospital administrators who want me to tell them who is authorized to visit my client in hospice. Unfortunately, I sometimes get inundated with the sordid elements of life. This occasionally happens when a person becomes ill and has not made decisions on two key things. Number one: Who has medical power of attorney giving them authorization to make medical decisions for the sick person? And, number two (believe it or not): Who is the person who can decide who can visit the sick person? Ponder the following better-than-a soap-opera real life drama.

The Story Of Bill Bigshot

Although he never ran for political office, Bill Bigshot was the unofficial mayor of his city. Nothing of real significance happened in that city without his presence, approval or influence. He was in to everything, both civic and unsavory, and had the uncanny ability to keep the unsavory under wraps. The twice divorced millionaire and father of two sons was a businessman extraordinaire with ten successful businesses and plenty of women auditioning to be the third Mrs. Bill Bigshot. He managed to keep the women at bay, causing all kinds of wild speculations about any woman seen with him with the slightest degree of frequency.

The Bigshot Kingdom came crashing down the day Bill was hospitalized after being in a near fatal car accident. His extended hospital stay was no less than a circus with people coming and going, trying to see Bill and guessing about his chances of survival. Or, should I say, people were trying to come and go? After all, Bill Jr., the oldest son, took control of the situation. While there wasn't much coming; there was a whole lot of going. You

see, Bill Jr didn't allow a lot of folk to visit his father and most visitors were shocked to learn they could not see Bill while he was hospitalized. No matter how close they felt they were to Bill, they simply weren't on the "visitation list" Bill Jr. created and were turned around at the door. And oh, I can't forget this part. Bill's family and friends didn't like how Bill Jr. was handling things; so, they started legal guardianship proceedings and had Brad, Bill's youngest son, appointed as legal guardian in order to strip Bill Jr. of his self-appointed authority. By the way, all of this was strange because, as one might suspect, the conscientious Bill Sr. already had a medical power of attorney for medical matters and a durable power of attorney for business and financial matters. None of the parties appointed in his legal documents were his children. Somehow, Bill's legal documents were abandoned once the legal guardianship proceedings began. Apparently, the persons appointed in the legal documents Bill prepared for himself were not interested in fighting Bill's children to fulfill the role of medical and durable power of attorney.

As if the drama of folk constantly being denied hospital visitation wasn't enough and the drama of people fighting to be medical power of attorney wasn't enough, two different women emerged for a hospital visit, each with a child they claimed was fathered by Bill. Bill Jr. knew neither of the women, but this didn't stop these unsavory hidden affairs from finally appearing and making their demands. The rumor mill was churning after a hospital hallway spat between Bill Jr. and one of the mystery women escalated. Hospital security was called as the woman shouted her demands to visit Bill Sr. and get money to support her child. This was not the first incident of its type.

Droves of people coming and going, sprinkled with clandestine women screaming child support demands, was way too much for the hospital to deal with. There was no way they could manage patient care in a hospital intensive care unit amongst that kind of uncouth belligerence! Therefore, all visitors, except for the two known adult children of Bill Bigshot, were banned from visitation! It was the only way to allow Bill to get much needed medical attention and to restore the proper work environment for an intensive care unit.

This is the likely outcome when there is a fight over who will be the person in charge of making medical decisions, or when visitation incidences threaten the peace of a hospital environment. When these types of events go unaddressed, they undermine the ability of the hospital staff to provide care to the patient.

Therefore, it is important to have a medical power of attorney that firmly establishes who is in charge and the scope of their authority. In addition, it is important to let family members know who the medical power of attorney is so that no one tries to usurp the authority of the appointed medical power of attorney when it is time for that person to act. Let's examine what a medical power of attorney is, why it's important and what you need to know to make a medical power of attorney useful and most effective.

What Is A Medical Power Of Attorney?

A medical power of attorney is a document that is often done in conjunction with a living will. The medical power of attorney gives another individual the power to make medical decisions for you. The living will is a document or part of a document that says whether you want to be on life support. Sometimes the medical power of attorney and the living will are done together in one document. So that you will understand different terms, be aware that a person who has medical power of attorney is sometimes called a healthcare surrogate. The healthcare surrogate, or medical power of attorney, is the substitute who will speak with a doctor on behalf of the person who is unable to speak with the doctor themselves.

Why Is A Medical Power Of Attorney Important To Healthcare Providers?

The medical power of attorney is extremely important to healthcare providers. Whenever a family member or friend must step in and make medical decisions for a person, it's better if the medical and hospital personnel know exactly who to talk to. There are many situations where someone is in the hospital and there is a lot of confusion about who oversees medical decisions. If a person has not appointed anyone as medical power of attorney, there could be a power struggle. Even if there is a medical power of attorney in place, there may still be a struggle and the hospital staff really doesn't want to or have time to referee the boxing match between people fighting to be in control. Consider the story of Bill Bigshot. The person noted as medical power of attorney in Bill's legal document did nothing, not wanting to fight with Bill's strong-willed oldest son. In the meantime, there were people trying to visit and getting turned away. There were spats in the hospital hallway with unknown women trying to get child support. For its own peace of mind, the hospital banned all but a very few visitors. Ultimately, the guardianship court ended up appointing someone to make medical decisions and handle Bill's affairs.

Even when there is someone to make medical decisions, there are often other issues regarding visitation of the person who is hospitalized that create plenty of controversy. Because fights about who can or cannot see a hospitalized patient are so common, the following is a description of what you are likely to see.

Hospital Visitation Cases Of Banned Visitors And Hostile Takeovers

Often disgruntled relatives look at each other when in a loved one's hospital room and whisper, "What is she doing here?" The "she" that they are referring to is usually someone whom they believe should not be visiting the sick person for any number of reasons. And then there is the visitor who agitates other visitors by asking the sick patient all kinds of outlandish questions or otherwise misbehaving. You would think that people would know how to conduct themselves when someone is critically or terminally ill. Wouldn't you know how to behave visiting a sick person in the hospital?

Well, it seems like some people just didn't get good home training. They were not taught proper manners for hospital visits. You wouldn't visit someone in the hospital whom you never related to outside of the hospital, would you? You wouldn't overstay your hospital visit, making it two hours rather than 30 minutes, would you? And you would dare not ask someone what's wrong with them, how long they have to live or whether they left you anything in their Will! I just know you wouldn't! Am I right? All these things I hope you wouldn't do are common occurrences. Therefore, instead of the medical power of attorney only making decisions concerning medical treatment, they should be authorized to make decisions and guidelines concerning patient visitation in hospitals. Moreover, it would make a lot of sense for the medical power of attorney to discuss this with the person who appointed them as soon as they find out they have been appointed medical power of attorney. In this way if there is a need, in the future, to make decisions about who can and cannot visit, there will be a basis for the decisions based upon prior conversations with the person who has been hospitalized.

To gain a better understanding of visitation challenges, let's consider some of the possibilities. When it comes to people's health care, I have seen four types of scenarios related to banning or allowing patient visits in hospitals. These are worth reviewing so that you can decide what should or should not be happening if you are ever hospitalized or appointed medical power of attorney.

Scenario 1-Banning A Specific Visitor. My phone rang about 11pm one night. It was a hospital administrator wanting to know who was authorized to visit someone in hospice. The administrator said that my terminally ill client's son had been forcibly removed from the hospital by the police. The son, at his mother's death bed, was demanding to know whether she left him anything in her Will. Sometimes unruly people cause such a ruckus when they visit, the hospital must ban them to restore and keep peace in the work environment. This scenario is the banning of a specific person. (This may be viewed as a drastic measure but I know of circumstances in which specific disgruntled people attempted to get the sick, emotionally compromised, hospitalized person to sign papers making them the new beneficiary in the Last Will or of life insurance!)

Scenario 2-Banning A Group Of Visitors Named On A List. Sometimes the hospital receives a list of people to ban, generated by a self-appointed person who never received medical power of attorney from the patient. This authority may have been given to the self-appointed person because they are who the doctors know and have been working with. Or, the one "in charge" may have actually been named power of attorney in a properly drafted and executed legal document. Sometimes the one "in charge" is well respected by the patient's family and brings unity. Sometimes the one "in charge" pulled a hostile takeover and appointed himself. Imagine arriving at a hospital and as you approach the patient's room, you are asked your name and told you are on the not-allowed-to-visit list! When your shock and anger wear off, you realize you now must submit to the one who ascended to power and assembled the list, even though you think the person is unauthorized. This scenario is the banning of a specific group of people who are on a list.

Scenario 3- Banning Of All But Persons Named On A List, Only People On The List Can Visit. Occasionally, because the hospital staff does not want the added responsibility of policing and banning certain visitors, the hospital will deny all visitors except for a limited number of next of kin or people on a list. Sometimes the hospital receives a list of people who are allowed visitation, and all others are banned. Here too, the list may have been created by a self-appointed person with no documented authority from the patient. The list maker may be hostile or well intended. Whatever the case, if you are not close to or regarded by the person who made the list, you may be considered insignificant no matter what your relationship with the patient. You may find yourself disappointed and banned. This scenario is the banning of all but a few people who are on a list of authorized people.

Scenario 4- No Ban, Everything Goes, Anybody Can Visit. A well known person lands in a local hospital. People are coming and going, in and out of the hospital room. The steady stream of visits is disruptive to the health care providers and allows the patient no rest. This is a situation where someone needs to draw boundaries and set up visitation guidelines. This scenario is a no ban, everything goes, unmonitored visitation policy.

How To Make Your Medical Power Of Attorney Useful And Effective

So that unauthorized people do not make self - appointments, giving themselves authority and taking control of your medical care, treatment surroundings and banning people you would prefer to see, you should do a medical power of attorney. Your medical power of attorney will authorize the appointed medical power of attorney to consult with healthcare providers, make treatment decisions, apply for healthcare benefits from agencies such as Medicare and Medicaid, authorize release of information to facilitate your care and authorize your admission or transfer to a medical facility. Although it is not usually done, be sure your medical power of attorney states how you want your visitors and environment handled if you want specific boundaries set concerning patient visits. And yes, if there are particular people or families that you don't want to visit you, say so. Even if you do not place specific names of people and families in your legal document you should make your wishes clear to your medical power of attorney. There are a lot of people who believe that the medical power of attorney only pertains to medical decisions and not whether a person has a right to visit a sick person. Some people believe that the medical power of attorney has no authority to deny them a hospital visit and may go as far as calling the police and demanding to visit, filing for a restraining order or getting an injunction against the medical power of attorney who denies them a visit. If you want to restrict visits or assure that certain people or family members are not allowed to visit you, make sure you seek legal counsel about the proper construction and execution of your medical power of attorney so that it is enforceable.

One final thing. It's good to have a medical power of attorney that says everything you want it to say about your care and visitation should you be hospitalized. But this medical power of attorney will do you no good if the person you appointed is harassed or usurped by someone who thinks he or she should be your medical power of attorney. This is what happened to Bill Bigshot. Although he had a medical power of attorney, his appointee never stepped up to assume the role, preferring instead not to get in the fray and to allow Bill's children to do whatever they wanted.

Be proactive. Protect the people you appoint to positions of authority. Once you execute your medical power of attorney and other legal documents, let the people you appointed know. Have a detailed discussion with them about your wishes. Most importantly, let the ones who would think they are to take control of your affairs know that you have appointed someone, and it is not them. Or, at least let your appointees know to be prepared to fight whomever comes to oust them on the basis that they are entitled to be in a certain position by virtue of biological relationship, regardless of the appointment in your legal documents. Be proactive. Your medical power of attorney should be given all the tools they need to serve when the time comes.

Questions You Should Ponder Before Doing A Medical Power of Attorney

1. Who do you want to make medical decisions for you? You should name a primary and an alternate person. You need to put a specific person in charge. This should not be done by a committee. Although it may be good for your primary designee to keep other friends and family informed, the primary person

should not be controlled by a committee. Otherwise decision making will be hard, and the health care providers may not be willing to convene committee meetings about your care.

2. Does the person you are considering as your medical power of attorney have the emotional stability, psychological strength, maturity, good judgment and intelligence to deal with a medical crisis?
3. You do not have to name your spouse or your oldest child as your medical power of attorney. Are you choosing a specific person, such as your spouse, out of duty and not because you think they are the best person for the role?
4. Is there any one you would not want to visit you if you were hospitalized? Most people have someone they don't want to come around if they are ill. In creating this medical power of attorney, you need to give your medical power of attorney written instructions concerning who you want to be in your presence and who should not be.
5. Do you know of any people who are unhappy with what you have in your Last Will & Testament, who you named as a life insurance beneficiary or who you have

given authority in your legal documents? Do you think that any of these unhappy people would sneak into your hospital room while you are sick and mentally or emotionally compromised and try to get you to sign documents they brought you, changing things to their liking and benefit?

6. Does your medical power of attorney know your position concerning life support? If not, tell them. They need to know your wishes.
7. This question should be obvious, but I will include it anyway. Does the person you intend to name as your medical power of attorney have your best interest at heart? Would they want you to hurry and die because you have left them something in your Will?
8. Do you plan to tell your next of kin who you named as power of attorney? If not, you should, especially if you did not appoint them. It is extremely important that you tell any person who thinks that they should be in charge but was not named as your medical power of attorney. This lessens the likelihood that the real medical power of attorney will be harassed by the person who wants to be in charge but was not appointed by you.

Decision 3

Do You Need A Durable Power Of Attorney?

What you are about to read may make you chuckle, or it may anger you a bit, but it is serious and wise legal advice. Never give power of attorney to your grandson who just got out of prison after serving time for fraud and theft. Never give power of attorney to the child who needs to feel like you trust them more. Never give power of attorney to the relative that you have had to support multiple times over several years. You may be surprised at the number of people who use unbelievably bad judgment when it comes to selecting a person to serve as power of attorney. I have had the unpleasant experience of working hard to fix bad situations created by people who gave power of attorney to the wrong person. Yes, one person gave power of attorney to her ex-convict grandson who was just released from prison!

What Is A Power of Attorney?

A durable power of attorney is a document in which you appoint someone to take care of your business and financial matters if you are unable to take care of them yourself. This document, in the wrong hands, allows a person with bad motives or in desperate situations to take your assets and do with them things you never intended for them to do. This document, in good hands, allows your agent to help you tremendously in the handling of your affairs.

Common Mistakes Associated With The Power Of Attorney

I have seen five common types of mistakes related to the durable power of attorney. One mistake is when power of attorney is given to the wrong person. The second mistake is when the type of powers given is too broad, not having been restricted to the specific activity for which it was intended. The third mistake is when the power of attorney is properly drafted and given to the right person but left open for challenge, causing the person appointed as power of attorney to end up harassed, challenged and even taken to court. The fourth mistake is when a power of attorney is given by a person who expects it to be operative after they pass away. And the fifth mistake is when a person waits too long before doing the power of attorney.

The Story Of Miss I Didn't Tell Him To Do That

This true story is a glaring example of two common mistakes with the power of attorney. It shows what happens when the power of attorney ends up in the

wrong hands, mistake 1. And, it shows what happens when the power of attorney is too broad, mistake 2.

Miss I Didn't Tell Him To Do That was ailing from multiple medical problems and decided to seek the help of her brother. She was told that she could simply get a general power of attorney from a local business supply store and did not need to incur the cost of hiring an attorney. Besides, doing a power of attorney seemed simple enough to Ms. I Didn't Tell Him To Do That. So, she bought the power of attorney form, checked every box on the form giving her precious brother the authority to do all kinds of transactions. She gave him the form with only her signature on it, instructing him to take care of her bills.

The brother was wise enough to realize the power of attorney still needed the signatures of two witnesses and a notary before he could do anything with it. Somehow, he was able to get them without his sister being present. (The execution of the document was faulty because it should have originally been signed in the presence of the witnesses and the notary). The brother then went give-me-crazy! He presented the power of attorney document to his sister's bank and cleaned out her account. He also used the document to put her property in his name! Miss I Didn't Tell Him To Do That was irate. She argued that she never authorized him to take her money nor her home and promised to sue the bank. However, and unfortunately, none of the attorneys she consulted were willing to take her case. After all, since she actually signed to give her brother power of attorney; on what grounds could she sue the bank and on what grounds could she sue her brother? Her only argument was, "I didn't tell him to do

that," an argument that may not carry that much weight in court. Besides, the brother had already spent the money and getting a judgment against him wouldn't be worth the paper it's on! And, putting him in jail wouldn't produce the money either! The brother knew that she would not have approved his actions, but there was nothing in her broad over-reaching power of attorney that restricted his behavior.

The Durable Power of Attorney authorizes the person of your choice to handle your financial and business transactions. This is an immensely powerful document and should only be executed after great deliberation and careful selection of a person you trust to give power of attorney. Some powers of attorney are restricted and are given for a specific person to perform only specific tasks. Other powers of attorney are broad in that they give the person you authorize to transact your business extremely broad leeway and authority to handle, in many instances, any transaction that you can handle. For this reason, you should be extremely careful who you give power of attorney because this person may be able to sell your property without your involvement, take money out of your bank account without your knowledge and any number of profoundly serious actions with dire consequences. Make sure you hire an attorney to do your power of attorney so that you clearly establish parameters, boundaries and guidelines that are easily understood. Make sure you trust the person you give power of attorney and be sure the person is not in financial dire straits and has shown integrity in financial dealings over the years.

Even when a power of attorney is property drafted and given to the right person, the person receiving power of attorney may be subject to harassment and challenges from family members who think they have too much power or who want to be power of attorney themselves. Usually if a person has a Durable Power of Attorney, it will suffice to place the intended person in authority. Occasionally, family members will still argue against a properly executed Durable Power of Attorney, say the document is not valid, create suspicion among those who want to rely on the Durable Power of Attorney and inevitably force a family to go to court to appoint a guardian.

I am reminded of a true power of attorney family feud. During this feud, an innocent person was attacked and taken to court only to find out that her Mom was wishy-washy in her decision making - to say the least. This is the third type of mistake commonly seen with power of attorney designations.

The Story Of A Family From The Wild

Grandma Wild was just as unruly as her children and grandchildren. She didn't have much money, so it was hard to understand why so many of her descendants fought to become her court-appointed guardian. The contenders thought they would get what little money grandma had. (The contenders did not realize they would not have carte blanche to spend Grandma's money as they choose.) One person said Grandma Wild did not want the person named in the Durable Power of Attorney. When Grandma Wild was asked if she wanted who she appointed in her legal document, Grandma Wild scanned the courtroom to gauge the faces of her most rambunctious children and grandchildren and then exclaimed, in open court, "Naw, I don't want her. I sho' don't!" This was a far cry from the mild mannered Grandma who came to my office, escorted by the person she made power of attorney in her document, and adamantly insisted that the documented person given power of attorney was clearly and irrevocably her choice. When the court asked Grandma Wild, "Well what do you want?" Grandma Wild said, with complete oblivion to the fact that she was not helping the situation at all, "I just want to go

home." Grandma's family was full of drug addicts and the people Grandma seemed to want to please at the court hearing were either chronically unemployed or of questionable character. The court ended up appointing a total stranger, a guardian that was never mentioned in the document Grandma prepared.

This brings us to a few points about what you need to know to make your Durable Power of Attorney enforceable. More than anything, your decision about who will be your power of attorney should be your decision and should be a firm, unwavering decision. There should be no signs that you were unduly influenced by any family member. For instance, have your discussions with your lawyer alone, without the people to whom you are giving authority. Go to the lawyer's office alone or ask someone who is not involved in the matter to take you to your lawyer's office. Pay your own attorney's fees. Do not allow your power of attorney to pay your fees. Firmly make your own decisions and do not vacillate under pressure from relatives. You know your family and you know whether it is likely that they will fight over your appointment. If your family is prone to fight, prepare and date your document and get a notarized letter from your doctor immediately saying that you were of sound mind when you drafted the document. In addition, it may serve you well to video the execution of the document and on the videotape, you should speak to your family about your intent and your wishes. When angry family members challenge your power of attorney appointment, the court will look for signs that the appointment was not valid or based upon undue influence. The outcome of court battles may be quite different from what you originally intended. Therefore, solidify your plans by making them clear, even to family members who may disagree. Use an experienced attorney to complete and implement your plan so that you are sure you have met all the statutory and legal requirements.

Another common mistake (the fourth) when it comes to a durable power of attorney is that people often think they can use the power of attorney that was given to them after the person dies. The durable power of attorney dies the moment the person who gave it to you dies. It is no longer active and won't give you any power after the person dies.

The final common mistake that I see is people tend to wait until they have become demented and they can no longer function, and then their family members go to an attorney and ask for power of attorney on their behalf. By this time, the demented person who needs to give the power of attorney no longer has the mental capacity to give it. It is then too late. If you are of sound mind now, this is the best time to do your power of attorney, even if you don't think you need it.

Questions You Need To Answer Before Choosing A Durable Power Of Attorney

1. Do you have any memory loss, signs of the onset of dementia or signs of Alzheimer's disease? If so, consult your physician to see if you have the mental capacity to do legal documents such as a power of attorney. Get a letter from your doctor saying you are capable of understanding and signing legal documents.
2. Who do you want to be the power of attorney?
3. Does the person you are considering have their own finances in order? If not, you are setting yourself up for

problems. Stealing your money and assets will be a temptation to try to solve their own problems. A hungry dog should not watch the meat house!

4. Can you trust the person you want to appoint as power of attorney?
5. Is the appointment of the person you are considering practical? Practically speaking, it's going to be difficult for a person to do something for you if they are in another state or in another country.
6. Have you created conflicting documents? When you give someone power of attorney to handle your affairs, you need to make sure you don't have other documents, like a trust document, where you made somebody else trustee over the same thing the power of attorney addresses. The trustee is different from your power of attorney, so you need to create your documents in a manner that there's not a conflict as far as who is in control of what and who can do what.
7. Is it your intent to allow your power of attorney to function only if you are incapacitated and cannot take care of your affairs? If your answer is yes, what you really want is a specially drafted springing power of

attorney which springs into action when physicians have certified by affidavits that you cannot handle your own affairs.

8. Have you determined the activities you want your power of attorney to do? Are they a broad range of activities such as handling insurance, business matters, banking and property matters or is it restricted to something like bill paying only? Be sure to give only the power that is needed to do the activity you intend.
9. Have you made provision for the handling of your affairs after you die by putting a Will or Trust in place? This is important because a power of attorney becomes inoperative when you die.
10. Have you taken measures to protect the person you appointed as power of attorney by videotaping the execution of your power of attorney? Did you make your choice known to people you know will challenge your appointment of a specific person?

DECISION 4

DO YOU NEED A LAST WILL AND TESTAMENT?

This is what famed artist Pablo Picasso said about himself:

> **"When I die, it will be like a shipwreck, and as when a huge ship sinks, many people all around will be sucked down with it. It will be worse than anyone imagines." (From Ariana Stassinopoulos Huffington, Picasso: Creator and Destroyer, New York: Simon & Schuster, 1988)**

Pablo Picasso foretold his legacy accurately. According to his biographer, Ariana Stassinopoulos Huffington, when he died in 1973, everything concerning him was in utter disarray. Although he had built an empire worth 260 million dollars, his personal affairs and relationships were in chaos.

The Story Of Pablo Picasso, Postmortem

Picasso had no Will so no one knew what was in his estate. He had three illegitimate children, by various mistresses, whom he hadn't spoken to in ten years and who were banned from his funeral. According to his biographer, he was estranged from everyone in his family except his second wife, Jacqueline. Many believe Picasso may have had mental problems. And the biographer's report that famed psychologist Carl Jung likened some of Picasso's painting to the drawings of his schizophrenic patients tends to support that belief.

It took five years of litigation to settle Picasso's estate because the mistresses, wives and their children were scratching and wrangling for their entitlement. During those five years, Picasso's prophecy that "as when a huge ship sinks, many people all around will be sucked down with it" began to come to pass. On the day of his funeral, his grandson swallowed a container of bleach and died three months later. Picasso's mother hung herself four years after his death. And his beloved ex-wife Jacqueline, the only one he got along with, shot herself in the head 13 years after his death. Mr. Picasso, you were right. This amount of tragedy and loss was surely "worse than anyone imagines."

Many believe that if a person has a Last Will & Testament, things will not be chaotic when they die. So maybe if Picasso had a Will, things would have been better. However, having a Will does not always prevent chaos. A Will can help the family of a deceased person, and the courts, understand the wishes of the departed loved one but the Will doesn't always prevent chaos. People sometimes challenge Wills in court and fight lengthy battles to have a Will declared null and void. And sometimes the reason people have court battles over estates is related to deep rooted psychological and relational problems that have existed for decades and cannot be fixed by a Last Will & Testament.

What Is A Will & What Does It Do?

A Last Will & Testament is a document that states who you want to handle your estate if you pass away and who will get the assets that you own at the time of your passing. A Will normally names family members of the deceased person and may even name a family member who is to receive nothing. Wills often have a brief section about the payment of debts of the person who signed the Will as testator and will have a section which names a specific person as the personal representative or executor of the estate. Usually there is language in a Will that defines what the personal representative is authorized to do.

The Last Will & Testament of a deceased person is filed with the court in the county in which the person lived, died or owned property, depending on the court rules in the area where the opening of the estate case is contemplated. The court receives the Will and uses it as a guide to carry out the wishes of the person who has passed away. When a person dies without a Will, the court then looks to the state statutes to determine how to handle the person's estate. Having to resort to the state statutes is not always good. For instance, if a person dies and has no spouse, three children and no Will, the state statutes will divide the decedent's assets among the three children equally. But what if it is well known that the decedent would not have given one of the three children anything. Well, the decedent would have needed to exclude this child by executing a Will, before he died, stating his wishes. If the decedent died without a Will, then the court will simply divide everything equally according to state statute. Thus, it is important to write your own Will and not allow the court to use the state statutes to decide how to distribute your assets.

So, what does a Last Will & Testament do? It gives the court guidelines from you with specific instructions as to who will be the personal representative and who will receive the assets from your estate.

What A Will Cannot Do

There are some things that a Last Will & Testament simply cannot do. In many states, you can't use a Will or some other estate plan to disinherit your spouse or a minor child. For instance, homestead laws in the state of Florida protect wives and minor children from losing the homestead property to another person. These homestead laws provide protection even if a deceased spouse wanted to give the property to someone else. Consider the following.

The Story Of Ms. Intelligencia

Ms. Intelligencia is an intelligent woman. She prides herself in being proactive and taking charge. She often speaks of how she is the only college educated person in her family and how she often has to provide guidance and leadership for her other siblings who often lose their way. Therefore, it came as no surprise that Ms. Intelligencia took control of her father's affairs to help him put his cheatin' wife in her place.

Long after Ms. Intelligencia and her siblings were adults her father, in his later years, married a younger woman. Ms. Intelligencia never trusted the gold digger with her elderly father and always believed that the child born to their marital union was not her father's child. She and her father vowed that they would fix this. To gain revenge from the grave, Ms. Intelligencia's father deeded his homestead where he lived with his young wife to Ms. Intelligencia. Shortly after the death of her father, Ms. Intelligencia filed the deed and let her father's young wife know that she was to vacate the premises. Unbeknownst to Ms. Intelligencia, her actions were totally illegal. The property deeded to her by her father was homestead property and could not be transferred to anyone other than his wife and minor child. The law in Ms. Intelligencia's state protects spouses from getting jilted and left homeless by deed transfers and Wills that leave spouses out. Ms. Intelligencia's estranged stepmother sued her, made her cancel the improper deed and made her pay all the attorney's fees associated with the lawsuit.

The moral of this story - consult an attorney to find out whether what you are planning to do is legitimate and legally permissible.

Make no mistake, spousal rights are real and enforceable. Just like a spouse cannot be deprived of homestead in the state of Florida, a spouse cannot be deprived of spousal rights even if they have been separated 20 years! People often expect emotional pleas about how long an estranged spouse has been gone to make a difference in court. It does not. Let the next story be a lesson to you. Don't learn this lesson in court. It won't be pretty!

The Story Of "Ms. Lucas"

Mr. Lucas and Ms. Lucas were faithful members of their church for more than twenty years. No one, but the church mother, knew that "Ms. Lucas" had never married Mr. Lucas. The sanctified church mother repeatedly insisted that she make this arrangement right and demand marriage. However, Ms. Lucas had grown complacent over the matter and was not up for the fight, seeing that Mr. Lucas had not married her after all these years. In fact, Mr. Lucas, being the fine upstanding minister of music that he was, steeped in denominational tradition, did not believe in divorce.

Therefore, he had not and would not divorce the real Ms. Lucas from whom he had separated five years before the new Ms. Lucas-in-waiting became his live-in woman. So, "the live-in woman but not wife," continued the arrangement, paying most of the bills including the mortgage on the home, since she always made much more money than Mr. Lucas.

Well, as fate would have it, Mr. Lucas died suddenly of a heart attack. Then came a cesspool of unresolved issues and the incessant "I told you so's" of the church mother. It turns out that the only name on the deed to the property was Mr. Lucas. Although the name of the estranged spouse was never on the deed, she was, nevertheless, his legal wife. And, you know the end of the story.

The only Mrs. Lucas came from California, sold the house and kept all the $60,000 made from the sale of the house. It did not matter that the live-in woman had been with Mr. Lucas for 20 years. It did not matter that the live-in woman had paid the mortgage all those years. Mrs. Lucas, the legal wife, came, collected the proceeds and headed back to Cali! Case closed.

Yes, people complained that this was not fair. But, the one who could have made things right and well, was gone. The moral of this story - don't assume that things will be done in a "fair" manner. Find out your legal options. Make a Will and other appropriate arrangements to protect yourself.

Key Things To Remember About A Will

Key things to remember concerning a Will are, first, if there is a Last Will & Testament, the family of the deceased person will have to go to court. Having a Will does not keep you out of court! Probate court is the only governing body that can authorize the transfer of the assets that were left to people in a Last Will & Testament. The process can take anywhere from six months to two years, even when there are no problems, fights or contested adversarial court proceedings.

Second, understand that doing a Will is inexpensive in comparison to the cost of doing a trust agreement, which can be expensive. If you do a Will, although inexpensive upfront, increased costs of administering that Will come into play when a person passes away and you must hire a lawyer to go to probate court.

Third and finally, remember that a Last Will & Testament is typically not private. Once a Last Will & Testament is probated, in many instances, you can go right to the court in the county and state where the probate case is opened and request information from that file, and even see the Last Will & Testament. If you're concerned about privacy, you may wish to consider other options, like a revocable trust, rather than a Last Will & Testament.

Mistakes And Misunderstandings When It Comes To The Last Will And Testament

Mistakes are common when it comes to the Last Will & Testament and are often associated with people trying to do their own. When people do their own Last Will & Testament, they think they are cutting costs. However, often they create situations where they end up paying a lot more money to straighten a big mess! Why? Inexperience and ignorance of statutes lead to the creation of something that was never intended. By the time the mistake in the Last Will & Testament is discovered, it is usually too late to correct it because the person who did his own Will has died. So that you can avoid the classic pitfalls concerning Wills, the following is a presentation of some of the most common mistakes and misunderstandings.

Creating Conflicting Documents. The creation of conflicting documents, such as designating a specific beneficiary on a bank account, and then creating a Will that says give the money in the bank to another person, is a quite common mistake. It causes confusion amongst beneficiaries when the Will is not the document that controls who gets the money. Even if the bank document is 10 years old and the Will was done a year before the person died, the old bank document is going to control who gets the money in the bank. Don't make the mistake of thinking that a recently done Will takes priority over an older bank beneficiary form. The bank is not obligated to adhere to a recent Will which they knew nothing about. Therefore, courts have ruled that banks only have to follow the beneficiary designation in their records. If you want to name a beneficiary for a bank account, do it at the bank and not in your Last Will & Testament.

Failure To Name A Guardian For A Minor Child. A quite common mistake is when people have minor children and they don't put any backup parents or guardians in the Will. If you have a minor child, you should always name a guardian for the person and property of that child in your Last Will & Testament. The guardian of the person and guardian of the property may be two different people. It depends upon who is best suited. Just because a person is suited to be a guardian of the person, responsible for the physical care of the child, does not mean they have to be the guardian of the property, responsible for handling the child's assets which could conceivably be a lot of money. Please bear in mind that if the minor child still has the other living parent, that parent has rights, even if he or she is a deadbeat. I have seen living parents challenge the right of the deceased parent to appoint a guardian, even though the living parent had shown no inclination whatsoever to take care of the minor child. Be sure to consult a lawyer about effective ways to remove the assets of your child from the hands of the other parent who is a deadbeat, if this is the situation you believe your child could face. This can be effectively done using a revocable trust to hold the child's assets and to appoint a responsible trustee who is not the deadbeat parent.

No Business Succession Plan. Another common mistake which creates great hardship for families is when people have businesses with no business succession plan. When a spouse who is a business owner or co-owner passes away; suddenly the surviving spouse may find out the family has no way to gain control of or get any money from the business that once took care of them. Without proper planning, the business may have failed to carry key man life insurance that would replace the deceased owner's income and help sustain the business as it recovers from the loss of its owner. Sometimes family-owned businesses are so poorly organized, no one knows who is in charge after the death of the owner and there may be very little information about how to keep the business going, especially if the heirs of the decedent were not involved in the business.

Failure To Understand Homestead Laws. Many times, people don't understand homestead laws in the state of Florida, and this can be the source of great confusion and even shock. If you have a homestead property and it's yours only, and you marry someone, they instantly become an owner too. There are a lot of people who say their new spouse's name is not on the deed or that they had the property before they married the new spouse. It doesn't matter, the homestead property - upon your death - will belong to the surviving spouse as a life estate when his or her name is not on the deed. This is shocking and disturbing to a lot of folk! Another shocker is that the surviving spouse, whose name is not on the deed, may be able to sell the homestead property and take proceeds from the sale!

Believing Your Absence From A Hearing Gives You Leverage. And, oh, I can't forget this one. Many people believe if they don't show up for a court hearing, the court and whoever started legal proceedings can't do anything against them or do anything at all. If you are a beneficiary or if you think you should be a beneficiary and you receive a hearing notice, consult a lawyer prior to the hearing, but most importantly show up. It is much easier for your opponent to get what they want if you keep quiet and don't show up to protect your rights. If you show up and argue your point, you have a much better chance of being given proper consideration.

Listing Bank Accounts In The Last Will & Testament. Inexperienced people often list bank accounts in Wills to name who they want to receive the money they have in a bank account. It is usually better to list a beneficiary with the bank where the account is located. In this way, your beneficiary will not need to go to court to get the money. If you list your bank account beneficiary in your Will and not with the bank, that beneficiary will face the unnecessary inconvenience of going to probate court and waiting a long time before the money is released to him. Even worse, a creditor may show up in the probate court case and fight the beneficiary for the money. You can circumvent this problem by simply listing a beneficiary with the bank.

Failure To Clearly Define Relationships. One final word about mistakes when it comes to estates and deceased loved ones, is don't be emotional. People often try to make legal decisions concerning estates based on pure emotions. They want the court to look at the closeness of relationships or whether the deceased was estranged from a relative or how long a couple was separated before a spouse died. Situations can be very emotionally charged when it comes to feelings about who is entitled to something from an estate. The court is not going to use charged emotions to make decisions. If someone is not a relative but of value to you, formalize your wishes by putting them in a Will. The fact that she was "like a" sister will not make her a sister when it comes to estate matters. Consider the plight of "Lika" (as in like a sister, like a daughter, like a son) in the story below.

The Story Of "Lika"

Lika was so angry. She couldn't believe what that lady did. That lady, Ms. Jones, had the nerve to file papers in court and become the personal representative of Lika's sister's estate. Well, Lika vowed to fix that. She filed papers in court to remove Ms. Jones from the court appointment as personal representative. Ms. Jones was merely a nosy friend trying to shut the family out and get all her sister's stuff. Well, sure enough, there was a court hearing and Lika prevailed by telling the court that Ms. Jones was a friend with no rights and no entitlement in the estate. But Lika was not ready for her surprise. Ms. Jones, being close to Lika's deceased sister, knew that Lika was not really a sister. Can't you imagine the dramatic soap opera music ringing in the ears of those in the hearing?

You see, Lika's dad had married the deceased woman's mother. Lika and the deceased woman had neither the same mother nor the same father. They were step-sisters of no biological relationship. Lika argued that this did not matter because she was "like a" sister to the deceased woman. Well the court didn't buy that. The court removed Ms. Jones from being personal representative then dug up an estranged legitimate half-

brother of the deceased woman to serve as the personal representative and receive the entire estate.

The moral of the story - "Lika" is not your relative. If a party has no actual biological kinship, do not try to create one based on your emotional attachment or closeness to a person.

You need a Will or an estate plan that is specifically tailored to carry out your goals. Remember, your Will or estate plan must be legally permissible, properly drafted and properly executed. Use an estate planning attorney. Otherwise, you may make needless and costly mistakes.

A Final Word About Wills, Will Contest And Personal Representatives

If a Will has been executed and you have been named the personal representative or are an heir of the decedent, there are a few things you should know.

If you are the personal representative, you should work very closely with your attorney and receive your attorney's instructions and approval before taking any action during estate administration. If the decedent has bills and you have access to the decedent's money, don't just start paying bills without instructions from your attorney because in many instances it is not necessary to pay them. Also, please understand that when a person is appointed personal representative that does not mean they can do anything they want to do. The person who is appointed personal representative according to a Will or according to state statute (if there is no Will) works under the supervision of the court and must seek approval for most - if not all - of what is done to administer the estate. In addition, the personal representative must protect the interest of the heirs and creditors of the estate. Before estate administration concludes, the personal representative handles making sure payments and distributions to creditors and heirs are done pursuant to court order and not according to his own wishes. I have emphasized this because some personal representatives are shocked when I tell them they cannot just do whatever they want to do with estate assets.

If you are an estate beneficiary, you have a right to be informed of what is going on in the estate and to take part in court proceedings. However, you must understand that sometimes people disagree with how the assets of an estate are distributed. While you are free to challenge a proposed distribution, your challenge must be based upon something other than you simply don't like what is going on. I recall a case I handled in which a daughter disagreed with her mother's Last Will & Testament and how the probate court distributed the assets. When the daughter was questioned about her position, she admitted that she knew the document was her mother's Will, but she just didn't like what her mother had done. This daughter felt that she should have received the same thing as the other daughter and nothing less. Well, again, the fact that you don't like what is in somebody's Last Will and Testament does not make it invalid. And, in case you don't know, your parents are not obligated to give you anything from their estate. They can choose to give everything they have to people who are not in the family.

And, let me make this clear. If you are a beneficiary in a contentious probate matter where there is a lot of fighting about who should get what, be reasonable. Don't spend $10,000 in attorney's fees to fight over an item that is worth $1000. Or, don't do a Will contest or trial and pay your lawyer $20,000 when all you stand to gain is $10,000. It makes sense to settle some things so that you don't go in the hole financially. When there is a family fight in an estate matter, be sure to consult an experienced attorney who can explain the pros and cons of your case, whether the fight is worth it, whether the law is on your side and whether there are enough assets to justify a fight. It's a sad day when a beneficiary says, "If I had known I wouldn't be getting any more than this I would not have gone to trial." Make sure you get a good understanding as to what's at stake before you jump into the boxing ring!

Questions You Should Answer Before Doing A Will

1. Have you ever drafted a Will yourself? If so, where is the Will kept and have you given other people copies? If you have given copies, to whom have you given them? You must share this information with your lawyer.
2. Do you realize your loved ones will have to go to probate court if you write a Will?
3. If your family must go to court to probate your estate, do you realize that the probate court file is not private?

4. Are you in an undefined relationship? Living together does not constitute married and separated does not constitute divorced. Separated means you still have a spouse who has legal rights to your estate. If you have a girlfriend or boyfriend and are still married how will you protect that girlfriend or boyfriend?
5. Who will serve as executor of your estate?
6. Who will serve as the alternate if the primary person named as executor cannot serve?
7. Would you like to keep your spouse from getting anything from your estate?
8. Do you have children or other relatives who are going to fight for assets when you die? If so, discuss the nature of these relationships with an attorney.
9. Who is your residual beneficiary?
10. Which assets are you giving away and to whom?
11. Have you created conflicting documents? For instance, do the bank records name one beneficiary while your Will names another for the same bank account? Do you have a trust that says one thing but a Will that says another?

12. Do you have minor children for whom you should name a guardian?

13. Do you own a business? If so, do you have a business succession plan?

14. Is there anybody you owe money whom you believe should be paid from your estate?

15. Do you have any people who are not biologically related to you, but they are like a brother, sister, son or daughter? If so, would you like to make provisions for them in your Will?

16. Who are the people you want to receive nothing from your estate and how are they related to you?

17. Who do you want taking care of your pets and have you provided funds for pet care?

18. Do you want to leave anything for your church or favorite charity?

19. Do you want any property to be sold and the proceeds divided? If so, who gets the money from the sale?

20. Have you written a program for your memorial service? Who should and who should not appear on the program?

DECISION 5

DO YOU NEED A REVOCABLE TRUST?

The Story Of Ms. Know It All

Ms. Know It All knows more than everybody. She is hard to reason with and hard to correct. She makes all her decisions from her vast wealth of knowledge and from consulting the ancestors. She decided, after burning candles on her ancestral altar and receiving from their infinite and immortal wisdom, to do her own legal documents. Surely with her intellect, and the otherworld knowledge of the ancestors, she's smarter than any lawyer and able to draft any document needed. So, Ms. Know It All decided one day that some family property needed to be transferred by deed. She dressed her ancestral table, placed a freshly baked cake upon it, lit candles and incense and asked for the steps she should take. She decided to set up a trust for a property owned by her uncle. It was his desire that Ms. Know It All and another relative own the property upon his death.

Well, some semblance of a trust document was created from a strange model that looked like neither a Trust nor a Will. Maybe the model document was from the other world. Perhaps Ms. Know It All didn't fully understand the instructions from the beyond. This sorta-kinda trust was then executed by the uncle. But there were no witnesses. No trust deed was done. This means the trust was never funded. Therefore, the property remained in the uncle's name only - per the original deed.

Years after the uncle died and became part of her ancestral table, Ms. Know It All decided since she was the owner of the property, she would use it as collateral to obtain a loan. Well, she was shocked and appalled when she learned that the hybrid Will/Trust she created was null and void! Why? Let's see - improper construction, lack of witnesses and lack of a trust deed signed by the uncle to put the property in the trust. Because Ms. Know It All's trust document was no good, she was told to probate her uncle's estate to get the property in her name so that she could obtain a loan. You know what? Ms. Know It All didn't believe she needed to do all that. So, Ms. Know It All, being as smart as she was, went back to the ancestors and came up with a posthumous plan to put the property in her name. She carried out her first posthumous plan by creating a deed in which she named herself trustee and owner of the property and signed the deed as the owner making the transfer to herself. The deed, not having come from the uncle, was rejected and Ms. Know It All was told, a second time, to probate the estate in court.

Being resilient and still believing in short cuts, Ms. Know It All launched her second posthumous plan to get the property in her name. This second plan was another deed, worded slightly different. This plan failed too, and Ms. Know It All was told again, a third time, to probate the uncle's estate in court.

Well, well! In dismay after being given such a hard time by all those people who demanded probate, Ms. Know It All reluctantly began probate administration! Because the uncle had no valid Will, there ended up being several intestate heirs, not just Ms. Know It All. Luckily for her, and I guess by some fortune of some ancestral intervention, all of the heirs thought Ms. Know It All already owned the property, knew how many years she had taken care of and invested in the property, and agreed to give her the property.

On a side note, Ms. Know It All often contacts me to look over other documents she drafts with the help of her departed ancestors. Again, I tell you, carrying the mantle, anointing and wisdom of the ancestors, Ms. Know It All knows everything. She knows more than everybody. Even me - her lawyer. (This I say, even after her ancestral documents were declared null and void and I had to clean up her mess!)

What Is A Revocable Trust?

Ms. Know It All created a mess with her trust. However, if you do a revocable trust properly, it can work wonders for you.

A revocable trust is a document that is prepared to create a legal entity that holds your property in the trust and helps you avoid going to probate court. When you create a revocable trust, it is a document in and of itself, but there are companion documents that go with it, such as the deeds that will place your property in the trust. This process of doing a deed to place your property in the trust is called funding the trust. You must fund the trust. Otherwise, your revocable trust doesn't work.

It is important to note that the person who creates a trust normally serves as the initial trustee. Then, if you pass away or become incapacitated, the successor you name in the trust will assume the role of trustee. Your successor trustee will transfer the assets in the trusts after you die to the parties you name in the trust.

Why Do Some People Prefer Or Recommend A Revocable Trust?

The trust is not like a Last Will & Testament which puts you in court, often in proceedings open to the public and gives the court control of the process of transferring assets to heirs. Therefore, some people prefer a revocable trust. The trust allows you to preserve privacy by avoiding probate and it gives you control over your assets. For instance, in many states, if a minor child is going to get assets from an estate, or insurance proceeds over a certain amount, you have to create a legal guardianship which is an ongoing court case that can last for years until the minor becomes 18 years of age. If you have placed the assets in a trust, then you don't have to create the guardianship. If there is a trust, then there is no court supervision of the trustees. If there's not a trust, but a Last Will and Testament, then everything that you're doing in the estate is under probate court control and supervision.

One of the most powerful benefits of a trust is that a trust carries on even after you die. Assets can stay in the trust, managed by a trustee you select, until your beneficiaries reach the age you want them to be when they inherit from the trust. This is the perfect plan for giving younger beneficiaries money in installments through a supervised plan so that the funds will be used wisely. Or, you can use periodic trust fund payments to a beneficiary whose income you would like to supplement. Another good thing about a trust is that if there is a trust beneficiary with problems that may dissipate his trust inheritance, you can keep the assets in the trust to protect them from creditors, predators, current spouses, ex-spouses and potential lawsuits. With a trust, you can provide for a loved one with special needs without causing them to lose their government benefits.

Remember, with a trust, you still have full control of the assets in your trust. As the trustee, you can do anything with your assets that you could do before you put them in your trust. You can buy and sell assets. You can change your trust or even cancel it. (That's why it is called revocable.) In summary, there are at least seven benefits of doing a trust: (1) A revocable living trust allows you to avoid probate at death. (2) A trust prevents court control of assets. (3) A trust provides privacy. (4) A trust allows for quick distribution of assets to beneficiaries. (5) A trust can be used to prevent unintentional disinheriting. For instance, a Will may give a property to a man whose death caused the unintended result of giving the property to his wife. With a trust, the property could remain in the trust for the benefit of the man and if the man died, the trust would not have to transfer that property to his wife. (6) A trust lets you keep assets in the trust where they are protected from creditors and irresponsible spending until you want your beneficiaries to inherit. (7) A trust is a tool that you can use to reduce or eliminate estate taxes if you are married.

What Are Common Mistakes People Make When Attempting To Do A Trust?

The common most detrimental mistake concerning trusts is that inexperienced people who try to do them often leave out the most important final step of funding the trust. Another common mistake is when the person preparing the trust chooses successor trustees who have no business and financial sense. Why leave the hungry dog to tend to the meat market?

The other serious error I have seen in trust matters is the co-mingling of trust assets with personal assets. If you are a trustee of a trust, you should keep the trust assets separate from your personal assets. I recall a true story of a lady serving as trustee of her father's trust. This generous lady took a loan on her personal property to renovate trust property. Once she got the trust property renovated, the beneficiaries of her father's trust did not wish to pay her back. They fought her in court and demanded transfer of the renovated properties to them. The trustee's difficulties were heightened by the fact that she had co-mingled her personal funds with the trust funds, she didn't keep all her receipts and she never kept proper records for the trust. The only thing she had in her favor was the unmistakable evidence that the trust never had any money, just dilapidated properties. Also, she could prove she personally borrowed money and it was clear that the money to do massive renovations on the trust properties had to come from the trustee.

If you have a trust or are the trustee of a trust, be sure to have a joint meeting with your attorney and accountant to make sure you are setting up and keeping your records properly and using the best tax saving strategy.

Questions To Answer Before You Do A Trust

1. Have you ever prepared a revocable trust?
2. Have you ever managed a trust before?
3. Are you going to do a revocable trust and serve as the initial trustee? If not, why not? Most people who do a trust will be the first trustee themselves so that they can maintain control of their property. Then if they become incapacitated or if they pass away, they name in the trust document who the successor trustee will be.
4. For what purpose would you like to create a trust? Probate avoidance, tax savings, provide income for the welfare, education and benefit of children and grandchildren?
5. What real properties are you going to put in the trust?
6. Will you place any insurance proceeds in the trust?
7. Will you place any money in trust?

8. Are there any assets other than real property, insurance proceeds and money in a bank account that you want to put in trust?
9. Do any of your insurance policies list minors as beneficiaries?
10. Who will be the successor trustees once you are not serving as the trustee?
11. Are your successor trustees financially stable?
12. Are you planning to make provisions for children and grandchildren by setting aside money in the trust?
13. Are any of your trust beneficiaries presently minors?
14. Are any of your trust beneficiaries financially irresponsible?
15. Do any of your trust beneficiaries have problems with drug abuse?
16. Do any of your trust beneficiaries have legal problems or an active court case?
17. Do any of your trust beneficiaries have a spouse or ex-spouse whom you would not like to get anything from the trust?

18. Do any of your trust beneficiaries fit the category of a special needs or handicapped person?
19. Once you've done the trust, will you take the necessary steps to finalize it and make it active by funding the trust?
20. Are you or will you be receiving periodic instructions from an attorney about how to manage the trust, so that you avoid co-mingling the trust assets with your personal assets and keep tax returns and business records current?

DECISION 6

DO YOU NEED A JOINT TENANCY DEED?

The Story Of Ms. I'm Not Hearin' That!

Ms. I'm Not Hearin' That had a healthy disregard for her daughter-in-law, whom we will call, Ms. Be Gone. To Ms. I'm Not Hearin' That, Ms. Be Gone was nonexistent. Although she had been married to her son for more than 20 years, Ms. I'm Not Hearin' That never managed to feel anything other than her desire for her daughter-in-law to just be gone. Ms. I'm Not Hearin' That knew that she wanted her son to own her property if she died. So, she reasoned that the easiest way to achieve this goal was to simply put her son's name on her deed. She wrote up a deed and made it from Ms. I'm Not Hearin' That to Ms. I'm Not Hearin' That and her son "Mr. I'm Not Hearin' That." She filed the deed in her county recording office and breathed a sigh of relief, the deed finally having been taken care of.

Well, years later, the son, Mr. I'm Not Hearin' That, died. His mother assumed that her son's death would create no major problem for her because she thought if he died, she would just own the property alone. The problem was, she did not realize that deeding the property to herself and her son meant that if either of them died, their part would go to their heirs. Well, when the son died, his part went to his one and only survivor, his wife who could not stand Ms. I'm Not Hearing That's guts!

I had the arduous task of telling Ms. I'm Not Hearin' That that the deed she prepared meant she and the hated daughter-in-law had co-ownership! Well, I did a lot of hand holding and explaining and re-explaining. I drew illustrations and spoke in the most elementary terms. It soon became clear to me that I was getting nowhere. After two hours of giving sympathetic explanations to the lady, she looked at me and said, "I'm not hearin' that." Clearly, she understood; but could not accept the reality that she now co-owned the property with a woman she could not stand - her son's wife. When Ms. I'm Not Hearing That tried to talk to her daughter-in-law about deeding her son's interest in the property back to her, the daughter-in-law said, in essence, "I'm not hearing that."

Ms. I'm Not Hearin' That created what is called a tenants in common deed. However, she intended to create a joint tenancy deed. The joint tenancy deed works wonderfully if you know how to draft one. For Ms. I'm Not Hearin' That's intentions to have been carried out, she would have needed to draft the deed as follows: from Ms. I'm Not Hearin That, a widowed woman, to Ms. I'm Not Hearin' That and Mr. I'm Not Hearin' That, her son, as joint tenants with full rights of survivorship. Leaving out the phrase "as joint tenants with full rights of survivorship" was a big mistake that caused Ms. I'm Not Hearin' That to not own the property alone after her son's death. According to law, she owned it with Ms. Be Gone, the daughter-in-law who refused to "be gone" out of her life and off her deed.

The moral of this story - hire an estate planning lawyer to draft your deeds, wills and trusts so that you can be sure your intentions are carried out.

What Is A Joint Tenancy Deed?

A joint tenancy is usually a deed. Sometimes it's a bank account with at least two parties. You could have several parties, and when one owner dies, the remaining party or parties own that property or asset, without having to go to court to be named the owner.

A joint tenancy deed is a legal document in which more than one person holds title to property. It carries with it the right of survivorship in the sense that if one of the owners die, the other surviving owner or owners own the property by operation of law. These surviving owners do not have to go to court, and they do not have to worry about the deceased owner's part going to the heirs of the deceased owner because the deceased owner's interest does not transfer to the heirs.

If you have property and you know who you would like to give it to, it may be simpler and less costly to prepare a deed and put your name and the other person's name together as joint tenants with the right of survivorship. In this way if you die, the other person will own the property without having to go to court. If the other party dies, you (and other survivors listed as owners on the deed, if any) will own the property without court involvement. This is an easy, inexpensive alternative. There are, however, certain disadvantages to this strategy. If you put another person's name on the deed to your property, you have made them an owner and will need their consent should you decide to sell or borrow against the property. Moreover, if you change your mind and no longer want them on your deed, you will need their cooperation to take their name off the deed. Therefore, you should be cautious when considering adding a name to your deed. Another warning is, if you place someone with severe financial problems on your deed, their creditors may try to force them to borrow money on the property to pay off their delinquent debts creating a mortgage you never intended. Or, the creditors of a person on the deed to your property may try to force the sale of the property to get the person's delinquent debt paid off. So, do your homework and find out a person's financial condition before you consider adding their name to your deed.

Mistakes People Make With Joint Tenancy Deeds

The most common joint tenancy mistake is people not understanding how to create the joint tenancy. Sometimes people will try to create a joint tenancy, but actually create what is called a tenancy in common. When you create a joint tenancy, the deed needs to say joint tenancy with right of survivorship. Most laymen don't know that, so when they create the deed, they just deed the property from themselves to themselves and the other person they want to add on. When they do that, it is not a joint tenancy with right of survivorship. It's a tenancy in common. With a tenancy in common, if one of those two people dies, the other surviving one does not own it by himself. The surviving owner now owns the property with the heirs of the person who died, and this is often not what was intended. Remember that a tenancy in common gives ownership to the heirs of the owner who died. A joint tenancy with right of survivorship cancels out the ownership of the owner who died and gives the property to the survivor.

Questions To Answer Before Doing A Joint Tenancy Deed

1. Do you know how the properties you presently own are titled? Are you the sole owner? Do you own jointly as tenant in common, joint tenant, or tenant by the entirety?
2. If you add a person to the deed to the property, are they going to give the property back to you should you change your mind? Remember, if you add someone, then change your mind about having them as a co-owner, that person will have to cooperate and sign another deed to come off the deed you originally created.
3. Does the person you are adding to the property have financial problems? If so, know that you may have problems with their creditors once you put their name on the deed to your property. Sometimes other people who are placed on a person's deed will have all kinds of issues such as child support, back taxes, or judgments. If you add someone to your deed, then this person with all those financial problems may create a situation where creditors are looking to use your property to settle debts.
4. Do you consider yourself an owner of a property from your ancestors that was never formally transferred to

you by deed or probate proceedings? In other words, do you own heir property with several other people? If so, this could come with many complications. Discuss this with your attorney immediately!

DECISION 7

DO YOU NEED A TOTTEN TRUST?

The Story Of The Smirker

Ms. Smirk was the oldest of four siblings and she knew full well what her father wanted her to do upon his death. Her father set up a Totten Trust, making her the only beneficiary of his $80,000 bank account. He expected her to get the money and divide it equally among herself and her three brothers. Well, her dad died and as time went on it was clear to the brothers, they were getting nothing. They couldn't even find out what was in the bank. Despite their demands for information, the bank told them nothing.

Finally, in a last-ditch effort to get some of the money, the brothers reported their sister to the probate judge. They told the judge, truthfully, I might add, that everybody knew the money in the bank was supposed to be divided equally. The judge's first response was kind and sympathetic as he explained that the money had a beneficiary, was not a probate asset and was therefore outside of the jurisdiction of the court. The brothers, very frustrated with the judge's seemingly casual posture, pressed the judge to order their sister to share the money. They couldn't imagine this judge not wanting to correct this gross injustice! The more they pressed the judge, the more agitated he became. Finally, the judge ended the hearing saying, "The matter is outside of the jurisdiction of this court! I don't know what you are going to do. If you think somebody got your money, call the police! It won't be dealt with here." The hearing ended with the judge's demeanor screaming, "Now get out of here and don't say another word about that to me."

The brothers left the courtroom empty handed and confused. And what about the sister with the big fat $80,000 securely resting in her own bank account? She left the courtroom with a smirk on her face! What's the moral of this story? A Totten Trust can do a whole lot of good or a whole lot of bad! Ms. Smirk could have done the good deed of dividing the money with her brothers, but the law did not require her to because she was listed as the sole beneficiary. Ms. Smirk chose to keep the money and will be forever "bad" in her brothers' eyes, although the law was on her side.

What Is A Totten Trust?

A Totten trust is a simple form, usually seen in banks, on which you name a beneficiary for a bank account. It is called Totten because the attorney who created it for the banks was named Totten. It is a regular pay on death designation form in the bank where you name who you want to receive funds in your bank account if you were to pass away.

Why Is A Totten Trust Very Important?

A Totten trust is extremely important because it allows you to control what happens with your money in the bank. If you have money in the bank and you named a beneficiary prior to your death, your beneficiary can go to the bank, present a death certificate showing that you have passed away, present their ID, and receive the money immediately. If you don't list a beneficiary, then the money in the bank must go through probate court. When it goes through probate court, the money becomes subject to creditors. When the money is subject to creditors, it is likely that it will be used to pay attorney's fees, judgments, hospital bills and other debts the person with the bank account had at the time of death. You can prevent allowing creditors to get the money in the bank simply by listing a beneficiary.

What Are Some Common Mistakes When It Comes To Totten Trusts?

One of the most common mistakes made, when it comes to a Totten Trust or the designation of beneficiaries on bank accounts, is when the bank account owner names one beneficiary and expects that beneficiary to share the money with other people. Sometimes the named beneficiary is honest, desires to carry out the wishes of the original account owner and will share the money as instructed. Sometimes the person named as beneficiary will refuse to share the money. So, if you have $100,000 in the bank and you want five people to share it equally, do not give the money to one person and expect that person to share the money with the other four people. Take the time to go to the bank and list each beneficiary and the percentage they should receive. If $100,000 is to be shared equally among five people then your beneficiary listing should say: Person 1 – 20%, Person 2- 20%, Person 3- 20%, Person 4- 20%, Person 5- 20%. Make provisions for the five people to be notified, after your death, that they are beneficiaries and allow them to go to the bank to get their own money.

Another quite common mistake is the creation of conflicting documents. For instance, bank records may say that an account has a beneficiary. At the same time, the bank account owner may have created a Last Will & Testament naming another beneficiary for that same account. No matter when the Last Will & Testament was done, it will not control what is on file at the bank. For instance, if a Will was done in the year 2019 saying give the bank funds to Jim but there is a beneficiary form at the bank from the year 2010 saying give the money to Mary, you may think that the terms of the Will control because the document is more recent. Such is not the case. The bank document controls who will get the money; in this case - Mary. Can you imagine finding out that you are in the Will to receive funds from the bank account, but you can't get the funds because your name is not listed on the bank documents? It is very confusing and very disheartening when there are conflicting documents and a person's expectations are not met, especially if they were counting on getting money they won't be receiving. Check your estate, banking and insurance documents to make sure you are not creating conflicts in the designation of beneficiaries.

Questions You Should Answer Before Creating A Totten Trust

1. Do you have beneficiaries on all your bank accounts?
2. Are the current beneficiaries still the ones you want to have the money?
3. Are there any minors who are listed as beneficiaries on your bank accounts? If so, consult an attorney to find out what you can do to circumvent the need for a guardianship in the future.
4. Have you listed one person as a beneficiary on an account with the understanding that this one person will share the money with several people? If so, why won't you list the other individuals as beneficiaries and allow them to receive their money themselves?

5. Did you list beneficiaries for bank accounts in your Last Will & Testament? If you have done that, you need to update your Will and remove those designations, because you do not want your bank accounts having to go through probate court.
6. Did you list beneficiaries for insurance policies in your Last Will & Testament? If you have done this, review your plans with your attorney and be sure you are not creating conflicting documents or needlessly causing the insurance proceeds to go through probate.

DECISION 8

DO YOU NEED LIFE INSURANCE?

The Story Of Ms. Hunt Down Shake Down

Ms. Hunt Down Shake Down has been this way all her life. When somebody dies in her family, she starts the "hunt down shake down." She literally hunts down any insurance policy holder and does her best to shake 'em down. In her mind, they owe the family those insurance proceeds. She surveys the family and picks out who she thinks has an insurance policy on the dearly departed loved one. Then she makes a nuisance of herself, calling from house to house, demanding to know if the victim of her wrath has an insurance policy they are hiding. She goes to the funeral home and directs the mortician not to give

anybody a death certificate without her knowledge because she needs to intercept their request and force them to bury the dead. There is a Mr. or Ms. Hunt Down Shake Down in every family. And you know what? Even in families with many educated people, it is hard to get them to understand that a life insurance beneficiary is not bound to use insurance proceeds to bury their dead relative.

Mr. or Ms. Hunt Down Shake Down always comes to mind when I think of insurance. That's because I sometimes get calls from the one hiding the insurance policy for help in getting a death certificate without the meddling family member knowing. The reality is, if you are the beneficiary on the policy, you don't have to use the insurance proceeds to bury the dead. Remember that! That insurance money is yours to do as you please.

Aside from these Hunt Down Shake Down episodes, there is much to consider when it comes to life insurance. First you need to understand what it is. Then you should find out how much you need and the common mistakes you should avoid.

What Is Life Insurance?

Life insurance is a product which will pay money to your designated beneficiary upon your passing. It is a product where you will pay a monthly or quarterly premium. You make the payments throughout the life of the insurance policy, and at the time of death, the insurance company pays whatever the policy amount is. There are several types of life insurance: whole life, term insurance, universal life and accidental death. Typically, premiums for whole life are higher but do not increase over time and the insurance lasts for the duration of your life if the premium payments are made. Term insurance is often much less expensive, but it lapses at the end of the term. If the term is ten years, the insurance ends in ten years. Accidental life insurance only pays to the named beneficiary if the insured person died by the type of accident described in and covered by the policy. Occasionally, beneficiaries are surprised when no money is paid on an accidental death policy after the insurer discovers that the insured did not die of a covered or approved accident.

What Should You Know?

Life insurance matters can sometimes be tricky. Therefore, it is important that you know the following four things. First, you cannot make a life insurance beneficiary bury the insured person who has died. If you will handle a person's burial in the event of their death, don't count on being able to get their life insurance beneficiary to pay the funeral bill. What if they don't? Then what? The second bit of information you should know is what kind of insurance you have. Is it accidental, whole life, term or universal? Some mistakenly believe they have term or whole life insurance with a death benefit of a certain amount. Their loved ones are shocked to find out they have accidental death insurance which will only pay if the insured dies from a certain type of accident within a certain period from the accident. The third piece of information you should know is if the life insurance policy premium is scheduled to increase in the future. It is not good to find out about the increase when the increase is drastic and beyond anything you can afford. If your insurance premium will increase you need to know in advance so that you can make the best decisions with your budget in mind and with an understanding of the likelihood that you can handle a premium increase. Don't find yourself forced to do without life insurance if you think you need it. Look at your options, including preneed burial insurance if you are concerned about coming to a place where a life insurance premium will not be affordable. The fourth thing to know is when your life insurance coverage ends. Some policies are term policies that last for a specific term and the term ends just when you need life insurance the most and are uninsurable due to health conditions. Be sure to find out when your life insurance policy ends so that you can better gauge whether it is the best policy for you.

How Much Life Insurance Do You Need?

Financial advisors say that the amount of life insurance that you will need is usually around seven to ten times your annual salary. To determine the amount of life insurance you need, consider your debts, income, mortgage amount and people you would like to help with educational endeavors. Life insurance should take care of any debts that you wish to pay upon your death, including a mortgage; and should supply income that your survivors may need to support themselves. It can provide funds for any children or grandchildren you would like to help with getting a college education or their first home, pay for their wedding or cover their welfare in general. You should look at life insurance as something that stabilizes your family and not as just something to pay for a funeral.

Common Life Insurance Mistakes

Having a basic understanding of life insurance can be challenging. So, you should be aware of some common insurance mistakes so that you can avoid them. There are ten mistakes you should avoid.

1. Don't rely solely on group life insurance from your job. If you leave the job you will probably lose the life insurance. Therefore, it is better that you keep independent life insurance, even if your job provides it. It would be sad to lose your job-related life insurance after you retire only to discover that

your age makes it difficult for you to buy life insurance with a reasonable premium.

2. Don't delay getting more life insurance if you think you need it. Many people know they need more life insurance, but they hesitate to do something about it. The longer you wait, the more the insurance will cost. It is well known that increasing age normally comes with increasing premiums. If you need more life insurance coverage, don't delay.

3. Don't buy the first policy you see. The premiums for life insurance policies vary greatly. Do your homework. Go online and compare prices. Compare the reputation of the insurance companies you are considering. It is likely that you can find a competitive price with a reputable company if you do diligence and search for the best deal.

4. Don't ignore the specific terms of the type of insurance you have. If you have term insurance, understand when the term ends and whether you will be insurable at the end of the term. If you have permanent or whole life insurance, understand how the higher premium will affect your budget long

term and evaluate whether you want the "investment" component of permanent insurance.

5. Don't buy insurance without first calculating how much you really need. The purpose of insurance is not just for burial. You may have an unpaid mortgage or other debts that may need to be addressed. What about funds to support or educate your spouse, children and grandchildren?

6. Don't name minors as beneficiaries on life insurance policies. If you die and your named minor beneficiary is still a minor, you are likely to have created a need for a legal guardianship. Most states have laws that may prevent the disbursement of insurance proceeds to a minor. In many instances the money does not automatically get disbursed to a minor's surviving parent or caretaker. A legal guardianship is needed, and this will entail years of court reporting and attorney fee payments until the minor beneficiary reaches the age of majority and can receive the money himself. If you intend for minors to be beneficiaries of your life insurance proceeds, it is better to send the

insurance proceeds to a revocable trust that you have created, one where you list the minor as a beneficiary of the insurance proceeds.

7. Don't name your estate as the beneficiary on your life insurance. If you name your estate as beneficiary, you are creating the need to open a probate case, submit the insurance proceeds for court supervision and have the court rule whether your insurance proceeds can be distributed as your estate's personal representative suggests. If you name a proper beneficiary (either a person or a trust) and not your estate, the insurance proceeds will go to the named person or entity without the need for any court involvement.

8. Don't own your life insurance policy if you have a large estate. If you have a large estate worth millions of dollars, it is not wise to own your own life insurance policy. This is because the amount of the life insurance proceeds payable upon your death will be added to the value of your estate and will increase the value of assets to be taxed. If you are someone whose estate is worth millions and

you have a large life insurance policy, consult with your accountant to determine whether another person or entity should own your life insurance to decrease your tax liabilities.

9. Don't keep your life insurance policy a secret. The way you handle your estate and life insurance matters is deeply personal. You should protect your privacy. However, if you pass away, someone needs to handle your estate and will need to know vital information about your life insurance. Be sure to tell one or two people the specifics concerning your life insurance such as the name and contact information for the insurance company, the policy number, the amount of the insurance and the beneficiary.

10. Don't forget to update your beneficiaries. Life circumstances change. Relationships change. Needs change. Plans change. Be sure to evaluate your life insurance policies once a year to determine if you still want the same beneficiary. Some people go years without evaluating their insurance beneficiaries. When this happens, it increases the likelihood that a named beneficiary may have died or may not be the preferred person for whatever reason.

Questions You Should Answer Before You Purchase Life Insurance

1. Do you have life insurance? If so, how much?
2. Is the life insurance through your job? If so, do you plan to purchase life insurance that is not connected to your job?
3. Who are the beneficiaries on your life insurance?
4. Do you need to change the beneficiaries?
5. If you have life insurance, have you told the beneficiary about the insurance or is the insurance a secret?
6. Do you know how much life insurance you need?
7. How did you determine how much you need?
8. Do you have enough life insurance to handle burial expenses, debts, family income, mortgage, and the educational needs of children and grandchildren?
9. Do you have enough life insurance to take care of your children (or grandchildren) until they are adults?
10. Have you listed minor children as beneficiaries on life insurance? If minor children are listed, then it is highly recommended that you place the insurance

proceeds in trust, so that you do not create a need for a legal guardianship.

11. If you have funds set aside in your life insurance policy for children and the funds are going into a trust, is the trustee you have named the best person for the job?

12. Have you checked to see whether the insurance that you have is accidental or regular insurance? Many times, people have accidental death insurance and when they die by natural causes, rather than an accident, the family is shocked to find out they have no insurance coverage.

13. Is it better for you to get term or whole life insurance? Why?

14. If you have life insurance, do you know if and when the premium will increase?

15. If you have life insurance, do you know when it ends?

16. If you have no life insurance and cannot afford it, have you investigated purchasing a pre-need burial policy?

A Final Word

Use the questions at the end of each chapter of this book as a guide for making decisions and thinking through what you want to do in your estate plan. Also, use the real-life stories as lessons learned vicariously. Trust me. You would rather learn from the mistakes of others than go through these agonizing things personally.

If you have read the chapters in this book, you should have a better idea of what is right for you and, in particular, things you want to avoid. Armed with useful information and a clear picture of your personal goals, your next step should be to get your estate plan done by a competent attorney who handles estate planning and probate cases. Do not use an attorney who does a lot of varying cases and only occasionally does a Will for somebody. That attorney may not have the knowledge or experience to create the best plan for you. Use an attorney whose practice consists mainly of probate and estate planning cases.

The following is a chart that summarizes the key things you should remember about each of the eight types of estate planning tools covered in this book.

ESTATE PLANNING SUMMARY CHART

*****	Planning Category	Planning Tool	Key Things To Remember
1	Incapacity Planning	Living Will	• states whether you want to be on life support • is different from a Last Will & Testament, is sometimes called advanced directive • should be done with a private attorney even if you did one in a hospital or doctor's office
2	Incapacity Planning	Medical Power of Attorney	• names a person to make medical decisions for you if you cannot make them for yourself • should address who decides who can and cannot visit you if you are sick • should be done along with a living will so person given medical power of attorney will know how the person who gave them medical power of attorney feels about life support
3	Incapacity Planning	Durable Power of Attorney	• names a person to do financial and business transactions for you if you cannot • is no good after you die, the person you appointed will not be able to handle your estate using the durable power of attorney after you die • this document gives the person you appoint a lot of power, you need to really trust them if you appoint them
4	Estate Planning	Last Will and Testament	• states who will be in charge of your estate and how your assets will be distributed • does not keep your family from having to go to court • executor or personal representative must act under court supervision and cannot do whatever they choose
5	Estate Planning	Living Trust	• is a document that allows the transfer of property without going to court • does not work if documents are not worded properly and complete (must fund trust) • is not the same thing as a living will, is the same as a revocable trust

ESTATE PLANNING SUMMARY CHART (CONTINUED)

*****	Planning Category	Planning Tool	Key Things To Remember
6	Estate Planning	Joint Tenancy Deed	• is a deed on which you add the name of a person you want to own your property if you die • will not work if the words on the deed are not phrased properly to describe a joint tenancy • requires that the person whose name you added to your deed cooperate and sign if you want to remove their name from the deed
7	Estate Planning	Totten Trust	• is the pay on death card or form at the bank on which you named a beneficiary for a bank account • a good way to give loved ones money from bank account because no court procedure is required, simply present death certificate for account holder, beneficiary ID and beneficiary gets the money • if this bank document conflicts with what is in a Last Will & Testament, this document will normally prevail, even if it is not the most recent document
8	Estate Planning	Life Insurance	• is a tool which provides money to a beneficiary when the person who has the insurance policy dies • the life insurance beneficiary is not required to use the insurance money to pay for the funeral • when deciding what amount of life insurance to purchase, one should take into account the average cost of a funeral, debts that will need to be paid, income that survivors will need, any mortgage that needs to be paid, college that needs to be financed and what the purchaser can afford

Once your estate plan is created, look at your estate documents at least once a year and decide if you want to keep them as they are. There are certain circumstances that should prompt you to revisit your estate plan to see if there are changes and updates you need to make.

Your plan should be reviewed at least once a year and, if necessary, after review, it should be changed to accommodate new goals and circumstances. The following events or life changes should always prompt a review of your estate and incapacity plans:

*Entering a new year

*Entering retirement

*New marriage

*Recent divorce

*Death of spouse, child or family member

*Purchase of property or sale of property

*Start of new business or entry into new business ventures

*Financial windfall such as winning the lottery or receiving a large inheritance

*Any change in relationship with a party who you have listed in your estate plan or incapacity plan (i.e. person is no longer close to you or becomes involved in criminal activity or has become a liability in other fashions)

*Moving to another state

*Children becoming 18 years of age

*Birth of a grandchild

And remember, never do your estate and incapacity plan yourself. Nothing takes the place of hiring an experienced estate planning attorney.

Customized Estate Planning Seminars

Attorney Williams offers estate planning seminars as a community service. These seminars are free to the public, unscripted, lively and interactive. They are full of stories and practical ways you can avoid legal problems and protect yourself and your assets. Attorney Williams welcomes invitations from churches, family reunions, organizations and groups, both large and small, who are interested in an estate planning seminar tailor-made for its audience. At these specially designed seminars, you will learn:

- 25 Things To Do To Set Your Affairs In Order
- What You Need To Know About Heir Property
- What You Need To Know About The Reverse Mortgage On A Deceased Love One's Property
- 25 Estate Planning Tips To Help You Avoid Legal Nuisances & Nightmares
- Tips On How To Keep The Nursing Home From Taking Your Property From Loved Ones

- Ways To Effectively Write Undeserving People Out Of Your Will
- Tips To Help You Avoid Common Pitfalls Associated With Debt Left Behind By Deceased Loved Ones
- Tips To Help You Avoid Common Pitfalls Associated With Papers Locked Away In Safe Deposit Boxes & Greedy Relatives Who Rush To Claim Or Seize Property As Soon As A Person Dies
- A Simple Way To Understand Federal Estate Tax Liabilities And Whether You Will Have A Federal Estate Tax Liability That Could Spell Disaster
- What You Need To Know About Doing A Last Will & Testament
- What You Need To Know About Living Wills
- What You Need To Know About A Medical Power Of Attorney
- What You Need To Know About A Durable Power Of Attorney

- What You Need To Know About A Totten Trust (Pay On Death Account)
- What You Need To Know About A Revocable Trust
- What You Need To Know About Life Insurance
- What You Need To Know About A Joint Tenancy Deed
- How To Avoid The Most Common Estate Planning Mistakes

To schedule a seminar for your group or organization, text or call 786-831-9483 or visit the website at www.attorneyvernitawilliams.com or www.vcwlaw.com

Made in the USA
Las Vegas, NV
04 November 2026

57424297R10081